Food Dudes

RAY KROC:

McDonald's Restaurants Builder

Joanne Mattern
ABDO Publishing Company

visit us at
www.abdopublishing.com

Printed in the United States of America, North Mankato, Minnesota.
092010
012011

 PRINTED ON RECYCLED PAPER

Cover Photos: Getty Images
Interior Photos: Alamy pp. 14, 21; Corbis pp. 11, 19, 27; Getty Images pp. 1, 7, 15, 23, 24–25;
    courtesy of McDonald's Corporation pp. 5, 6, 9, 11, 13, 17, 22

Series Coordinator: BreAnn Rumsch
Editors: Megan M. Gunderson, BreAnn Rumsch
Art Direction & Cover Design: Neil Klinepier

Library of Congress Cataloging-in-Publication Data

Mattern, Joanne, 1963-
 Ray Kroc : McDonald's restaurants builder / Joanne Mattern.
    p. cm. -- (Food dudes)
 ISBN 978-1-61613-559-1
 1. Kroc, Ray, 1902-1984--Juvenile literature. 2. McDonald's Corporation--Juvenile literature. 3.
Restaurateurs--United States--Biography--Juvenile literature. I. Title.
 TX910.5.K76M38 2011
 647.95092--dc22
 [B]
                            2010027897

Contents

A Born Salesman

Millions of people around the world enjoy eating hamburgers and fries at McDonald's. In fact, you are probably one of them! This restaurant **chain** started as a simple idea. But Ray Kroc grew it into a huge, successful business. Today, McDonald's is a fast-food giant.

Raymond Albert Kroc was born in Oak Park, Illinois, on October 5, 1902. His parents were Louis and Rose Kroc. Louis worked for a communications company called Western Union. Rose was a homemaker and a piano teacher.

The Krocs did not have a lot of money, but Ray had a happy childhood. He grew up with a younger brother and sister. They were Robert and Lorraine. Ray enjoyed playing with them. He also liked playing baseball with other neighborhood children.

Ray was close to his parents. He loved watching baseball with his father. Rose began giving Ray piano lessons when he was six. He enjoyed music and became a very good musician.

From the time he was a young boy, Ray was good at selling things. He ran a lemonade stand in front of his house. Later, Ray worked in a grocery store and at a **soda fountain**. He and his friends even started their own music store. This early work set Ray on the path to becoming a successful businessman.

Ray (right) *was close to Robert* (left) *and Lorraine* (center).

Growing Up

Ray in uniform

In Oak Park, Ray attended Abraham Lincoln Elementary School. Later, he attended Oak Park and River Forest High School. Ray liked **debate**, but he was not very interested in schoolwork.

Then in 1917, the United States entered **World War I**. Though he was just 15, Ray wanted to help the war effort. So, he lied about his age to join the American Red Cross.

Ray went to Connecticut, where he trained to be an **ambulance** driver. He hoped to travel to Europe and help soldiers who had been hurt in battle. However, the war ended before Ray could go overseas.

After the war, Ray returned to school. But, he left after just a few months. Then, Ray got a job selling ribbons. At night, he played piano with **jazz** groups. Ray soon took a job playing in a band at a dance hall. It was near Paw Paw Lake, Michigan.

In 1919, Ray met a woman named Ethel Fleming. Ethel's parents owned a hotel in Paw Paw Lake. Ray and Ethel had fun together and soon fell in love. They married in 1922 and moved to Chicago, Illinois. In October 1924, the couple welcomed a daughter they named Marilyn.

Ray trained to drive ambulances alongside businessman Walt Disney.

Moving Around

Kroc needed steady work to support his new family. So just before his marriage, Kroc took a job with the Lily-Tulip Cup Company. He sold paper cups to restaurants and **soda fountains**. Kroc soon became one of Lily-Tulip's best salesmen.

Kroc also kept up with his music. He became the musical director for Chicago radio station WGES. Kroc hired musicians, played the piano, and performed with singers. He enjoyed this work.

Before long, Kroc wanted a new opportunity. So in 1925, he moved his family to Fort Lauderdale, Florida. There, Kroc began selling **real estate**. At first, business was great. But by the next year, sales had fallen dramatically.

Kroc needed to find another job. He began playing piano in a Florida club. Meanwhile, Ethel missed Chicago. So, Kroc soon moved his family back home.

Back in Chicago, Kroc returned to the Lily-Tulip Cup Company. Selling products was what he did best. Soon, Kroc became the Midwest sales manager.

Kroc learned a lot about business during the early years of his career.

The Multimixer

One of Kroc's Lily-Tulip customers was businessman Earl Prince. Prince owned several ice cream shops in Chicago. He had invented a machine that could make five milk shakes at once! Prince called it the Multimixer.

Kroc told Lily-Tulip about the Multimixer. He thought the company should sell it. But to his surprise, Lily-Tulip was not interested.

In 1939, Kroc made a big decision. He knew the Multimixer was a good product. And, he had always wanted to own his own company. So, Kroc quit his job at Lily-Tulip and started the Malt-A-Mixer Company. He began selling Multimixers to ice cream stands and other restaurants.

Kroc was a clever salesman. He even invented new drinks for his customers to make with the machine. By the late 1940s, Kroc was very successful. He sold more than 9,000 Multimixers a year in cities around the country.

The Multimixer led Kroc toward his opportunity with McDonald's.

Meeting the McDonalds

During the 1950s, times were changing. More people were moving out of cities and into **suburbs**. They no longer walked down the street to small ice cream stands. Instead, they drove several miles to large **chain** restaurants. As ice cream stands went out of business, Kroc began losing customers.

Yet, one customer was giving Kroc a lot of business. A small restaurant called McDonald's in San Bernardino, California, used eight Multimixers! The restaurant was owned by two brothers, Maurice and Richard McDonald. Kroc was curious about why the restaurant needed so many of his machines.

So in 1954, Kroc went to California to visit the brothers. McDonald's was unlike any restaurant he had ever seen. The building was tiny. People lined up outside to order food from a walk-up window.

The menu listed only a few items. McDonald's sold hamburgers, cheeseburgers, French fries, milk shakes, and soft drinks. Each item was prepared and served very quickly.

The original San Bernardino McDonald's

Kroc told Maurice and Richard their restaurant was a great idea. He suggested they expand their business into a **chain** of restaurants. But the brothers did not want to take on such a big responsibility.

First Franchise

Kroc did not give up on his idea. He offered to start a restaurant **franchise**. The three men agreed that Kroc could use the McDonald's name. In return, Maurice and Richard would get a percentage of Kroc's sales. In March 1955, Kroc started a franchise company called McDonald's System Inc. To get Kroc started, the McDonald brothers taught him how they ran their restaurant. They gave him the operating manual to their Speedee Service System. This system had an **efficient** setup in the kitchen. It was what allowed the brothers to prepare food so quickly.

Speedee was McDonald's original mascot. He represented the Speedee Service System.

On April 15, Kroc opened his first McDonald's restaurant in Des Plaines, Illinois. It was just like the one in San Bernardino. The restaurant had a small menu with cheap prices. French fries and sodas cost 10¢ each. Hamburgers were 15¢ and cheeseburgers were 19¢. Milk shakes cost 20¢. On the first day, Kroc made just over $366.

Kroc worked hard to make his restaurant a success. He wanted the restaurant to

The Des Plaines McDonald's became known as No. 1. Today, it is a museum.

be clean and attractive. Kroc often picked up garbage from the sidewalk outside. He told workers that the most important things to remember were quality, service, and cleanliness.

Building a Business

Kroc's dream was bigger than one McDonald's restaurant. So, he helped other people set up new McDonald's restaurants. Kroc sold 18 **franchises** in the first year. By 1957, there were 40 McDonald's restaurants in the United States.

Having the same name was just the beginning. Kroc wanted customers to have the same experience no matter what McDonald's they visited. So, franchise owners had to follow many rules. For example, they could only sell the products Kroc told them to.

In addition, all McDonald's products had to be prepared the same way. So, the French fries were always cut to the same size and thickness. The hamburgers were always cooked for the same amount of time.

Some of the McDonald's franchises did very well. One restaurant in Waukegan, Illinois, ran out of buns on its first day. Before long, the Waukegan franchise owners were making more money than Kroc was! Kroc realized he needed a better plan to make the most of his business.

Kroc partnered with Fred Turner (left) to develop his operating system for McDonald's.

The Big Sale

Kroc's next step toward success was asking businessman Harry Sonneborn for help. Sonneborn told Kroc to set up a **real estate** company for McDonald's. The company bought land that **franchisees** could rent to run McDonald's restaurants on. This system made a lot of money for Kroc. It also let him choose the locations for new McDonald's restaurants.

In 1960, Kroc decided McDonald's was successful enough to make a few more changes. He sold the Malt-A-Mixer Company. He also changed the name of McDonald's System Inc. to McDonald's Corporation.

By the next year, McDonald's had grown to include 228 restaurants. Kroc still had to share his profits with the McDonald brothers. He decided he did not want to do that anymore.

Kroc wanted to buy the rights to the McDonald's name and its Speedee Service System. The McDonald brothers agreed to sell for $2.7 million. Now Kroc had complete control over the company.

Also in 1961, Kroc started a McDonald's training program. He called it Hamburger University. All **franchisees** had to attend. There, they learned how to do things the McDonald's way.

By 1963, McDonald's consumers had eaten 1 billion hamburgers.

Getting Creative

During the 1960s, Kroc opened restaurants all over the United States. McDonald's restaurants also expanded to other places, including Canada and Puerto Rico. No matter where they were located, the restaurant owners had to follow Kroc's rules.

However, Kroc also let **franchisees** suggest new ideas. Lou Groen ran a McDonald's in Cincinnati, Ohio. In 1962, he created the Filet-O-Fish sandwich. It was the first addition to the original menu. Jim Delligatti was a franchise owner in Pittsburgh, Pennsylvania. In 1968, he wanted to add a bigger sandwich to the menu. So, he developed the popular Big Mac sandwich.

Sometimes, even Kroc tried to invent new menu items. One of his ideas was the meatless Hulaburger sandwich. This sandwich had a slice of grilled pineapple and two slices of cheese on a bun. No one wanted to eat the Hulaburger! So, it quickly came off the menu.

Today, McDonald's offers a wide variety of menu items.

Dessert Menu

McFlurry $4.58
OREO
$2.29

Cones $1.88
Vanilla .99

Shakes $3.58
TRIPLE THICK $1.99 $2.99
Chocolate • Vanilla • Strawberry

Sundaes $2
Hot Fudge • $1 each

Premium Salads

Choose CRISPY or GRILLED chicken.
NEWMAN'S OWN
All-Natural Dressings

California Cobb

Bacon Ranch

DISNEY PRESENTS PIXAR PALS

Ask about Toddler Toys for kids under 3

new Happy Meal choices

Happy Meal
Hamburger $
Cheeseburger $
4 pc. McNuggets $

Mighty Kids Meal
Dbl. Cheeseburger $
6 pc. McNuggets $

Choose apples or fries
Choose a drink

HAPPY MEAL	MIGHTY KIDS MEAL
HAMBURGER 2.59	DBL. HAMBGR. 3.49
CHEESEBURGER 2.69	DBL. CHEESEBGR. 3.59

Extra Value Meals / Breakfast

Meals include hash browns and a small coffee.

1. Egg McMuffin $3.89 Meal — Sandwich $1.89
2. Bacon, Egg and Cheese Biscuit $3.49 Meal — Sandwich $1.89
3. Sausage McMuffin with Egg $3.49 Meal — Sandwich $1.89
4. Sausage Biscuit with Egg $3.89 Meal — Sandwich $1.89
5. Sausage Biscuit $2.78 Meal — Sandwich $1.00
6. Bacon, Egg and Cheese Bagel $3.79 Meal — Sandwich $2.69
7. Steak, Egg and Cheese Bagel $4.19 Meal — Sandwich $2.79
8. 2 Sausage Burritos $3.49 Meal — 1 Burrito $1.00
9. Bacon, Egg and Cheese McGriddles $3.59 Meal — Sandwich $2.30
10. Sausage, Egg and Cheese McGriddles $3.59 Meal — Sandwich $2.39
11. Sausage McGriddles $2.48 Meal — Sandwich $1.59
12. Hot Cakes with Sausage Platter $3.59 — Served as shown
13. Big Breakfast Platter $3.59 — Served as shown
14. Deluxe Breakfast Platter $3.88 — Served as shown

Make it an Extra Value Meal!

Medium meals include medium fries and medium soft drink.

Large fries and large soft drink add 50¢ to meal price

D. Big Mac $4.89 Meal — Sandwich $

7. 2 Cheeseburgers $4.89 Meal — 1 Sandwich $

3. Quarter Pounder with Cheese $4.89 Meal — Sandwich $

4. Double Quarter Pounder with Cheese $5.69 Meal — Sandwich $

5. 6 piece Chicken McNuggets $4.79 Meal — Made With White Meat — Sandwich $

6. Chicken Selects $5.19 / $6.19 — 3 Pieces $3.29

D. Crispy Chicken $5.19 Meal — Sandwich $

8. Chicken McGrill $5.19 Meal — Sandwich $

9. Filet-O-Fish $4.89 Meal — Sandwich $

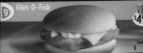

SANDWICHES

BIG MAC.

HAMBURGER .99 CHEESEBRGR.

QUARTER POUNDER. with cheese 2.89

McNUGGETS. 6 PC. 2.59 10 PC. 3.
CHICKEN SELECTS. 3 PC. 3.19 6 PC.
CRISPY CHICKEN 3.29 CHICKEN

FILET-O-FISH.

FRENCH FRIES
SMALL 1.00 MED 1.69 LRG 2.0

PREMIUM SALADS
BACON RANCH 3.49 or
CALIFORNIA COBB 3.89 or
SIDE SALAD

BEVERAGES
Coca-Cola Sprite
SMALL 1.00 MEDIUM 1.39 LARGE
SHAKE 1.79
COFFEE/HOT TEA 0
CAPPUCCINO/HOT CHOCOLATE 1.29
ORANGE JUICE 1.00 1
APPLE JUICE BOX 1.00 BOTTLED
LOW FAT MILK CHOCOLATE or W

Just for Kids

Kroc wanted McDonald's to be a family-friendly restaurant. So, he made sure it was a clean, happy, affordable place to eat. McDonald's began advertising these features on television and in magazines.

In 1963, the company introduced a popular character named Ronald McDonald. He was a clown who loved to play and be silly. Ronald McDonald quickly became one of the most recognized children's figures in the world.

The original Ronald McDonald

Kroc also worked to create a welcoming experience for children at his restaurants. Many restaurants had indoor or outdoor play areas where children could have fun.

Starting in 1979, parents had another reason to bring their children to McDonald's. That year, the company began offering Happy Meals. Each meal included a hamburger, French fries, a cookie, a drink, and small toys. Children loved these meals made just for them.

Kroc believed the customer's happiness was important to running a successful business.

Part of the Community

McDonald's made Kroc a wealthy man. He enjoyed using his fortune to help others. Over the years, Kroc donated much money to help children and families in need.

Kroc also knew what it was like to live with **diabetes** and **arthritis**. So, he started the Kroc Foundation in 1969. This organization raised money to fight these diseases. The foundation also fought **multiple sclerosis**, which Kroc's sister had.

In 1972, Kroc turned 70 years old. For his birthday, he decided to give $7.5 million to charity. Some of the money went to the Kroc Foundation.

Kroc also encouraged his **franchisees** to help others. In 1974, several McDonald's workers opened a special house in Philadelphia, Pennsylvania. Families could stay there while their children were treated at local hospitals.

Other McDonald's employees worked to open these houses in other areas. They became known as Ronald McDonald Houses. In 1984, Ronald McDonald House Charities was officially established in memory of Kroc. Today, there are more than 200 houses worldwide.

Visits from Ronald McDonald help cheer up sick children staying in the hospital.

Beyond the Arches

Kroc retired from McDonald's Corporation in 1973. However, he stayed active on the **board** of directors. And, he spent time with his family. Kroc had divorced Ethel in 1961. The next year, he married Jane Dobbins Green. Then in 1968, Kroc married Joan Smith. He became the stepfather to her teenage daughter, Linda.

In 1974, Kroc bought the San Diego Padres baseball team. Whether the team won or lost, Kroc enjoyed attending games in his free time.

Several years later, Kroc suffered a **stroke**. After this, his health continued to fail. On January 14, 1984, Ray Kroc died in San Diego, California.

McDonald's has changed a great deal since Kroc opened the first **franchise** in 1955. Today, the company is one of the greatest business success stories in the world. There are about 33,000 McDonald's restaurants in 118 countries.

Ray Kroc did not invent the hamburger or the fast-food restaurant. However, he made fast food **consistent**, convenient, and fun for millions of people around the world. His simple idea forever changed the way people eat.

Kroc's determination helped him find success.

Timeline

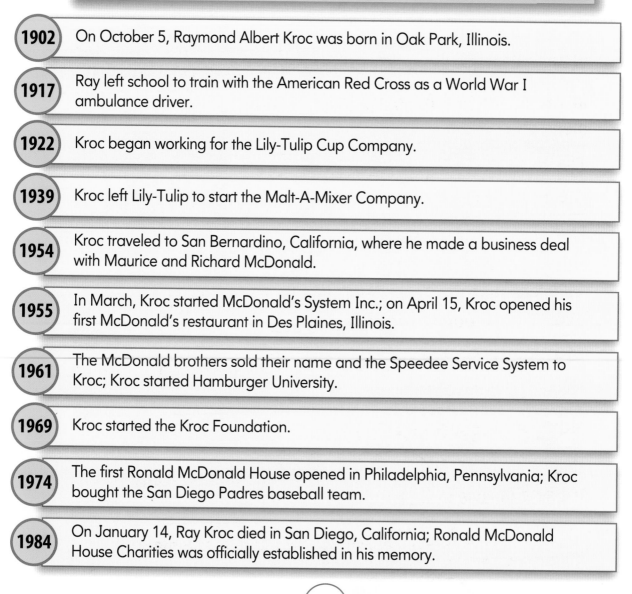

1902 On October 5, Raymond Albert Kroc was born in Oak Park, Illinois.

1917 Ray left school to train with the American Red Cross as a World War I ambulance driver.

1922 Kroc began working for the Lily-Tulip Cup Company.

1939 Kroc left Lily-Tulip to start the Malt-A-Mixer Company.

1954 Kroc traveled to San Bernardino, California, where he made a business deal with Maurice and Richard McDonald.

1955 In March, Kroc started McDonald's System Inc.; on April 15, Kroc opened his first McDonald's restaurant in Des Plaines, Illinois.

1961 The McDonald brothers sold their name and the Speedee Service System to Kroc; Kroc started Hamburger University.

1969 Kroc started the Kroc Foundation.

1974 The first Ronald McDonald House opened in Philadelphia, Pennsylvania; Kroc bought the San Diego Padres baseball team.

1984 On January 14, Ray Kroc died in San Diego, California; Ronald McDonald House Charities was officially established in his memory.

Menu Milestones

McDonald's is much different today than it was in 1955. Over the years, many milestones have contributed to this change. What do you think the next big idea at McDonald's will be?

In 1968, the Hot Apple Pie dessert became a standard menu item.

The Quarter Pounder and Quarter Pounder with Cheese sandwiches were added to the menu in 1973.

The Egg McMuffin sandwich was invented in 1971. This was the first McDonald's breakfast item. The full breakfast menu was available by 1976. Today, breakfast accounts for 15% of sales.

In 1975, the first McDonald's drive-thru opened in Sierra Vista, Arizona.

Chicken McNuggets were created in 1983.

Salads were first introduced in 1987. Premium salads became available in 2003.

In 2010, McCafe Real Fruit Smoothies joined the menu.

Glossary

ambulance - an automobile that carries sick or injured people.

arthritis - a medical condition of the joints that causes much pain.

board - a group of people who manage, direct, or investigate.

chain - a group of businesses usually under a single ownership, management, or control.

consistent - free from variation or contrast.

debate - a contest in which two sides argue for or against something.

diabetes - a disease in which the body cannot properly absorb normal amounts of sugar and starch.

efficient - able to produce a desired result, especially without wasting time or energy.

franchise - the right granted to someone to sell a company's goods or services in a particular place. The business operating with this right is also known as a franchise. A franchisee is someone who operates a franchise.

jazz - a style of American music featuring lively rhythms and melodies. Musicians often make up the music as they play.

multiple sclerosis (MUHL-tuh-puhl skluh-ROH-suhs) - a disease that affects the nervous system. It is marked by muscle tremors and eventual loss of muscle movement.

real estate - property, which includes buildings and land.

soda fountain - a store with a counter for preparing and serving sodas, sundaes, and ice cream.

stroke - a sudden loss of sensation, voluntary motion, and mental activity. It is caused by the breaking of a blood vessel in the brain.

suburb - a town or village just outside a city.

World War I - from 1914 to 1918, fought in Europe. Great Britain, France, Russia, the United States, and their allies were on one side. Germany, Austria-Hungary, and their allies were on the other side.

Web Sites

To learn more about Ray Kroc, visit ABDO Publishing Company online. Web sites about Ray Kroc are featured on our Book Links page. These links are routinely monitored and updated to provide the most current information available.

www.abdopublishing.com

Index